Tarot

Tarot

Jake Arthur

TE HERENGA WAKA
UNIVERSITY PRESS

Te Herenga Waka University Press
Victoria University of Wellington
PO Box 600 Wellington
teherengawakapress.co.nz

A catalogue record is available at the National Library
of New Zealand

ISBN 978-1-776-92137-9

Printed in Singapore by Markono Print Media Pte Ltd

What should such fellows as I do crawling
between earth and heaven?

—*Hamlet*, act 3, scene 1

Contents

Querent (I)

My dear, you're on a threshold,
I see. It's not hard to
When you have eyes:
Three of them.

But you're here and that
Signifies. Sit down, have a cup
Of tea. We're not above tea.
Leaves? Yes, but not today.

Tell me what you know about
Symbols. What does this mug
Mean? Does it mean to drink?
Does it mean hot? Or careful?

I can tell you're a sceptic.
Boys like you usually are.
It's childish, you know,
To be so sure. That one's for free.

One more. If I ask your name,
I'm asking *how* you say it. Where
You look. The way your hands
Go to your pocket, your hair. See?

That's easy magic. Some's harder.
God isn't physics, it's Fortune.
Fortuna: a woman and a wily one.
If you throw this dice, what number

Lands? There's maths for that, isn't there?
I'm waiting. Throw it just right
And get a five. Go on. Bad luck!
A six is no closer to five than one.

You're impatient, I can see. But
We can only begin when you look
At this plate and see the moon,
And in it your mother's face.

Can you do that? Well, let's see.
Here are the cards. Put your hand on them,
Close your eyes. You don't want to?
But you are blind with them open.

Switch off that brain of yours.
It's very loud. It's like a very white light.
This isn't surgery; this is a reading.

Receipt

or Ace of Cups

One bonnie day
As me and the marquesa
Got haptic in my dad's Cherokee,

I watched a dove
Fly past the rear windscreen
Carrying a letter.

What dispatch was that?
I felt that usurper Thought deflate me
And begged off a retreat.

She said, What the fuck?
Her concern was reciprocated.
There were not doves round here.

And if it was a nuncio, where
Was the court? I was thinking it was
The Holy Spirit, corresponding.

It was very sunny and hot,
The river was gay and so was the yellow grass.
Chins were getting ice cream on them.

The marquesa wanted to dip her feet,
So I knelt and gave her the Maundy
And saw two sparrows doing the same.

The spell
or Knight of Swords

No doubt women's names acted on me;
It was a phenomenon, a registering event,
Mary, Maria, Maryanne, up and down the staff,
Their illicit letters ran out to finishing sharps—
This, all my life, was normal;
Men's names, the Marks, the Toms,
The Jonathans, they didn't even decibel,
Like, if a mouth could moan them
Mine wasn't calibrated; it was out of range;
It was subject vs. object: I guess these guys
Made girls do it in a corner of my hard drive,
End of, *ne plus ultra*—but it wasn't, there was more;
He found me so gently where I was,
And manning lone that no-man's land,
What exquisite traps he laid out
By being himself, swapping letters from
Won't until it was Will, spelling no *y-e-s*;
He taught me a language I didn't want
To ever learn and waited for me to speak it;
I think he was confident; I think he knew;
He worked on me like a sentence
He just had to finish.

His mien

or Ten of Pentacles, reversed

No accounting her taste
For hangdog men, weak
Of chin and short in smiles,
Not so much brooding as broken,
And if he's good in the bedroom

No one wants to imagine it.
She's a giver, her bridesmaid says,
And it's true she has a thing
For belaying God's worst climbers.
But to be smitten with one?

Once she stopped by my desk,
Saw the photo. My sister, I explained.
And you, she said, You were a looker.
So she *does* have eyes in her head.
Are, she corrected, a bit too late for my pride.

Well, we're bequeathed youth
And slowly it's repossessed,
Like a reverse equity mortgage.
You marinate in your own juices
And the whole lot gams up.

Thing is, this guy's spirit levels
Were underground at conception.
Meanwhile some of us have
More hair on our bald pates
Than he has *joie* in his *vivre*.

Rest and recreation
or The Empress

His chest is a golden plate
Where she sees herself back in ridges
As though aged by the prospect of him.

But that's what young lovers are for,
Says her clever friend, the professor,
Whose lovers have never aged,
For *thinking about how far we've come*
. . . and how many times. Cue laughter.

When she draws back the curtains in the morning,
His back is laid out like a conquered world
She's not sure what to do with. Oh God,
Might the mattress be older than him?

He is very chipper today.
She keeps saying these fogeyish words
She never normally uses. Mustn't say
That his bottom in the shower is copacetic.
(Though it is. She even likes his huge legs.)

It's cruel to keep them too long.
The professor again, on the rights of animals
And sports scientists in their 20s.
They get (pulling a waa-waa face) *attached.*

But she feels rebellious. She has read about
And browsed photos of Sam Taylor-Johnson
(Poorly disguised envy in women's magazines)
And Brigitte Macron (merely French).

She is part cured when he of the golden chest
Gives her an unsolicited refresher on the ATP cycle
After which she is sure he is actually a PT,
And not a scientist of any kind.

But he *is* very sweet,
And it's so lovely to be a bit patronising,
And to be eaten out.

The robin
or Nine of Pentacles

A bird alights on her finger
As if by magic; the guests coo their pleasure,
Her finger a marble twig, party to
The robin's red ensign.
The trick has been a success
And for it gracing her finger
She looks the more beautiful,
The more diaphanous,
Not flesh, a vision.

But consider: birds have very small brains.
They are like a cashew nut, the meat of an acorn;
To teach them to do the trick, to do anything,
Is trying in the extreme, is an act committed
To the absurdity of things.
It says: yes, why not? Why not
A spectacle with a bird?

Why not use up this bird's short life
In taming it, in tempting it down from the tree
Day after day to make a habit, and draw it closer
To the waiting girl, the seed closer to her hand,
Then in it, then laid on her finger, until the bird hops on
For the first time? Then to stop it startling
When she moves? And the greatest trick of all:
To remove the seed, but for the robin still to come,
To fly over and wait, obedient on the finger,

Just because that is what it has always done,
Though there is nothing there for it,
Why not?

But, if it is all as absurd as I say,
Why then does the girl look so beautiful,
And the bird so proud?

Bird of passage
or The Fool

He had a knack for earthly love,
So keen he wanted no other masteries.
Yet he had them: in storytelling,
Mischief, cards, and persuasion.

A bird of passage with a light step,
He was a fisherman's nymph made man.
He drew O-shaped mouths his way,
Never letting them take a bite out
That he didn't want out.

But it wasn't his nature to be miserly;
His solar attention thawed everyone.
For women he had roguish grins,
A strong suit in kind words and
Dark corners to say them in.

Men he won first as followers
With table-thumping songs and tall tales
Before yielding soft and fey to the
Quiet, comely lad who most admired
The sovereignty of his noise.

Oh, what a wanderer love made him.
Novelty was his hunger and it wore
Thin with his patience, his heart as full
One moment as it was empty the next.

A nomad with a full itinerary
There were always pastures new, and no time yet
To look at what he'd won on the way.

Play-time

or Five of Pentacles

Where's that gas smell coming from?
She wondered this as her hands
Tipped the jerrycan over like
A stubborn bottle of ketchup.

Her brain and body were like
Cars flooring it in opposite directions,
And it had been like that a while.
Just a minute, sweetie.

It was November and cold, just dawn.
Her daughter with Olaf printed on her jacket
Waved at an Amazon truck kicking slush up.
She heard zilch and was dressed for May.

The cold she saw only as a fact relating
To the gas can, to the plan not being finished yet.
The last bit, what was it? Hard to think
With the house staring at her.

Places had personalities, ways of making
You think a particular way.
Just walking out of it she felt less fried,
The air or something, the cold air.

Moooooooooom.

A hollow *boing* and there was the can,
Emptily rolling on the ground.
And there was the wood pile, glistening,
There, next to the side of the house.

She saw the world was just facts coming in.
One after another like in a boring book:
This is what this is, that's where that is,
Her eyes kept sending her one after another.

You dropped it, Mom. Well, duh, she thought.
The schools didn't teach them anything now.
They taught Critical Race Theory. They taught
People to be ashamed. Who needed to be taught that?

She shut her eyes and only then she felt
The matchbox, in her left hand. The whole time?
A little game started between her head
And her body: to light it not looking.

She'd played that one a lot with her sister.
Tie your shoes blind. Blind, walk to the kitchen.
It was good to play. Adults didn't play, not right.
You could get sick of their funny games.

Lessons
or Three of Swords

The school was tawdry.
Nature photography, kids' posters,
Items of clothing everywhere
Left like props, placed.
It was hard to believe
Here was where anyone began.

The teacher thanked us again
For being there. She said,
We need to get onto their level,
Meaning the kids'. I thought:
Wasn't the point that they get onto ours?

We were sat in the pygmy chairs,
Appraising, being appraised.
The principal, we were told, was coming.
Like a bought-off journalist
My husband asked a patsy question
The other parents tittered at.

I frowned down a vestigial feeling,
By nibbling at the millimetre lip
Lasered onto my styrofoam cup.
By the door, stuck up under
'Student of the Week',
Was a child's self-portrait,
And crayoned in its corner,
A version of my own name.

Casement
or Nine of Swords

I woke
To a summer night,
Over-full from the feast,
Embers still in the brazier.

The very air was stuffed,
Steeped with cures, burnt spikenard,
Sleeping breath and the dying flowers
My attendants had pressed
Into my bedclothes, to heal me.
Cousin Eli snored next to me,
Curled inwards like a cat.

I pushed aside the heavy layers and got up,
My gown clinging see-through like a bed-wetter's.
The shutter beckoned:
Meadows, maidens, scenes of life.
It depicted what it kept from me.

I reached my hands
Into its moonlit slivers
To the cooler air behind
That tickled my fingers
With real maidens, living meadows.

'Cousin,' whispered Eli from the bed,
Alert and crouched in the dark.

Look up
or The Hierophant

I had a boy's trance for what muscle
Could do to the world:
He'd carry suitcases over his head
And dunk baskets just tip-toed;
These feats had a moral quality,
They said he was better, that he was right.

And he did stoop to form me,
He said *yeah* and *nah* in patterns
I internalised. I looked at him
After other people spoke, to check.
He'd nod, or tilt his head, or just
Ignore me, lesson in itself.

Don't do what I do.
OK, I said.
I don't know shit.
OK, I said.

He could be hortatory, or haughty.
I didn't mind. He'd earnt it. At times,
All alone, I saw him in the mirror,
And at the new house we had adjoining
Rooms, beds sharing sides of a wall,
His nearness, like a crystal, healed.

Once, he told me he was born
Yesterday, but I didn't get it.

He would end up riddling,
Trying to say what he meant.
This isn't a holiday to me, he said,
Walking me to the dairy for a Sprite.

He kept asking:
What do you want to be?
But I wanted to be a *who*, not a *what*.

In the future I had different eyes.
I watched my every move.
I stooped to get beers out of the fridge.
I carried suitcases over my head.

Palanquin

or The Sun

My agency is very frantic.
It goes everywhere, into other people,
Into their agency. This is called
Envy, hate and love.

I am one unlikely receptacle
Making space for desire—
Serial with the past and future,
Parallel with the present.

All mornings I wake
To the despotic myth called me.
Like smoke, you can look twice and
Not see it, and it can choke you to death.

I am not alone in here.
I'm a person peopled
By a booming mental population.

But of them all I'm my secret favourite,
I am in love with my agency the most,
My desire the most, my smoke the most,
Most my myth, most my inward boom.

Lost bantam

or Page of Wands

The island's sallying rocks,
An eyeful of white tops caught too late
By the men on the dusk-drawn deck.
The hue and cry when it did come

Was stillborn, a kind of scream
That curdled in the screaming,
Pitching from alarm and surprise
Down to lowing lament.

Just before, at the starboard lip,
Jim's guts were again being rocked up and out.
He stared fish-eyed at black nothing
Before another eructing gurgle.

The hurdy-gurdy of his sealegslessness
Had become his shipmates' favourite tune
To ape, in the bunks or at pissed dinners.
They wobbled after him, chest-heavingly effete.

But maybe the meek are saved?
With a sudden crack, the world broke its hinges
And the ship whipped forward and
Cast Jim praying into rockless sea.

*

That the dawn still had him in it
Felt like a new dispensation, like
The red sun was hung out just to dry him,
Not alone on the shore, but the only living.

Jim spent a day amid the wreckage
Prodding for life and later for provisions,
Marking the faces of his many antagonists,
Bloated and wan, dead out of spirit.

He tripped through whorls of branches
To drink brackish water and sat hungry
And alone on an outcrop, hearing birds
And waves louder than his thoughts.

His fortunate feelings died with the light.
He crouched behind fronds at noises
Never located, helloed phantoms, got turned
Over and over by eldritch thoughts.

He knew the map of the world was complete
But here he was on an oversight,
A slip of land by a slip of the pencil
Freckled onto the globe's spinning face.

And what if it was the Rapture, the elect
Sluiced from the deep instead of inhaled to heaven?
And if there were no ships to save him from being Saved?
And alone, what good was being good?

*

But he wasn't alone. He was woken
By a poking boot attached to a man
Otherwise gambolling in his god-givens,
As pale as an oyster, and half red rash.

Jim gave him quivering ministrations
With crushed-up dock leaves and
Failed reliably to avert his eyes.
Camping in the lee of the outcrop,

Stings soothed, this Pete, the Irish deckhand,
Fell into a chatty, smiling sleep.
So many muscles in a face, Jim thought,
Falling too, in his own doomed way.

The dawn crowned two peaks, the outcrop
And the still-sleeping deckhand's mast,
Nudging out their duvet of ferns.
Jim endured evil breath to stay very close.

Desire made him sleepless.
The punishment was so exquisite,
It had to be divine. Hell was sandy,
But in other particulars accurate.

It was Jim's luck, or God's, that just as he finally
Dozed off, Pete woke lazy and happy, a dog
With a bone, and brought himself off,
Wiping his fingers through the sand.

*

Then there was the morning and the matter
Of what to do with it. Pete prayed a rosary,
Licked dew from leaves, and went foraging
For what the dead wore.

Jim stayed inside his thick head,
Wandering Eden like it was the bad end of town,
Watching up for falling coconuts, down for
Beasts riding on their bellies.

He had been unhappy on the ship,
Unhappy on the shore. Back home
His mother said he'd been born under
A melancholy planet: he forgot which.

A bad seaman, a worse bartender,
Apprentice to the barber bad at lather,
And a good hunch, too, that he was bad at adventure,
Having not heart nor head for peril.

Sure he'd not see Pete's lovely pale bottom
Again, he cherished the outline
It made in its new linen encasements
As they hiked the hill for a lookout.

Self-pity dented his pace but when
Pete turned and saw his sad familiar
Leaning the way of the palms, he teased him
Before lifting him, light load, onto his back.

Necklacing, ashamed to grip,
Pete took the uncertain hands in his
So Jim's arms were like two reins:
A happy rider and an eager steed taking
The hill in stride, champing at the bit
And suddenly warming to not being found.

Flash

or Ace of Swords

The trip to Boulder Beach and
Torchlight sliding over sleeping faces—
You were there.
Yours was one of them.

Bedsheets rustled, and branches,
In wake of the already gone on,
The passed: like a helicopter over the bush.

In wake
To what you think you saw,
To what might've seen you.

Charity

or The Devil

My outfit was making me
Feel post-human, with an engorged
Sense of being at the centre of things.
I felt there was swivelling of eyes,
Eddies of attention redirecting.

I needed this hebdomadal boost
Like I needed to pay the rent.
It was, like, obligatory; it was like eating.
Get your fangs out, girl, advised the fag
To my hag. He was pretty sure
Vamping it up could cure cancer.

Maybe he was right?
I was walking down this street
And thinking he was.
I felt like a slutty handmaiden
To capital, to Mr Monopoly himself,
Euphoric in my new bra and knickers.

Was it *good*? Was it feminist?
Who put those two flies in the ointment?
Someone uglier could do the accounting.
I was busy making eye contact with strangers
Like I was giving alms to the needy.

They were so grateful
And I so full.

Goose
or The Moon

Justin was letting himself go rabbinical
In the beard, looking to pick up
Jewish fathers dropping their kids
At the yeshiva down the road.
Deep-seated issues, he declared,
Are the best aphrodisiacs.

I looked at him: full muscle Mariam.
OK, I said, but what if they ask you
About the Old Testament? He snapped:
They don't call it that, darling. I know
That much from Madonna.

I let my expression query this and slumped on his bed.
He was quite the sight, disporting himself
In the altogether except for a negligee,
His hairy chest a faux undergarment.
This was the man I was in love with

Hopelessly, though he was ridiculous.
Though I sometimes didn't even like him.
Though he was a faggy fag and my own
Deep-seated issues were more tradie
Flopping cock onto Formica.

Still, the heart was less superficial. And
More. Being in love had made me more
Self-conscious than ever. And now, what,

I had to convert? Like Charlotte
In *Sex and the City*?

Justin, I gestured pathetically. Hug.
He turned (he twirled) and gave me
An arch look. You goose, he said in Eton
And came over and kissed me, *mwah*,
You know you're my only real *abba*—

That's Daddy in Jewish. I pulled him into
Me and smelled his women's perfume,
Pushed up between his rough, iron pecs.
Darling, darling, he crooned, don't be silly.
I'm too much man for you. I'm a package
Deal. Not sold separately.

But we love each other, don't we?
Yes, I said. Yes.
He said, Now, where are my boots?

Man alone

or The Hermit

He could see himself
As someone else's flunky
Or driver, or fix-it man.
Maybe for a footballer
Or billionaire or rapper.
He'd drive slick cars,
Have a custom phone
And tailored suits, Italian.
He'd speak in nods and shakes.
He'd be scary ripped.

Long hours and only
Home a few nights a week
To his apartment, just his,
Fitted out like a barracks—
Maybe in a Dubai skyscraper—
Minimal like the stresses
He'd shed with his suit.
He'd walk naked on the
Deck, feel the day's heat
Give out, look down, way down,
And maybe scroll Tinder,
And always sleep like a babe,
No clouds in the desert,
No one on his case and just
Focused, just carrying out the plan.

Visit

or Ten of Swords

Mum had this glower and lour
She played up when the family came down.
It was a role you sensed she relished.
Arriving and the curtains were cinched up, spotlight on,
And *scene*, and *scene*—it must've been planned;
The beats were there, we were in our places.

She would enter hasting us to dinner, as if
It might walk off, as if we might otherwise idle to death.
What pressure does to pleasure: this was her study.
Her beautiful life was pinned like a calendar
In all four corners, stretched, and tense at it.
Strain came off her like heat, like her life was burning.

You learned to want to scream at a perfect entrée
Or at the simplest request, asked in tones of niceness.
She could do that. She could do more than that.
My sister said there wasn't proof, *Like, point to it*,
But that was her modus: she could deny you
Under the dining table or, livid, shush you to sleep.
The way that mask never broke, it was like a face.

Oh, Mum. Mother.
Love was there: it was all somehow for love.
You had us and we owed you.
We owed you the world.

Hasp

or Six of Coins

Just sex? Again he read it,
Staring down his phone with
Bright windows in his eyes
Empanelled by the oblong.

Just sex? It tore the hasp
From his lockless heart.
He was having this holy feeling
Popped like a bauble.

Then the phone went face-down,
And its owner's face turned up,
Making gravity pool to not rain.
What a baby, what silly swain.

But that man had so held him,
Just so. And just what did that mean?
Was it merely, was it hardly?
Rusty, russet, his ringleted hair

And an iron temperament, strong,
He thought, even when it weathered,
A heavy metal laid over him
To hold him steadily in place.

He was in a habit of honouring,
And he'd honoured him, begun to,
Turns out too soon. But was it wrong
To feel quickly, to get inundated

Like a biscuit in a cup of tea
And, hot and wet, to melt, crumbling?
No, he felt so strongly it was good
To just love, and not fight the feeling.

No—but others could not let themselves go.
They held tight to themselves. They closed
Fast, locking their hearts
Against a world of lovers.

What hast thou done?
or Seven of Swords

What made you man?
I was sure you were girl.

What thought disturbed
That limbic pool
And tipped it?

What made you shine your shoes,
The yellow lightbulb on in the garage,
The nugget blackening
Your child's hands?

Where were you that day
—the 15th of August 1998—
When you skipped double science
And got home 24 hours later,
Pale and wet as whitebait?

I can't be everywhere at once.
I can't see inside your head.
I can't always watch.

But mysteries make me uneasy.
Everything I don't know feels
Like a secret kept against me.

The universe is so vast.
It has many dark places.
Must you make another?

Vigil

or The High Priestess

The greater shadows
Slide from the valley
To your many-sided face—
Just as they did in ancient times
When the sun was new and you
Were a mote in the gloaming—

I might kiss you
On the cheek, on the bristles of your cheeks,
But for the sake of the light falling just
Right—

In this same dusk a shepherd
Took up his glinting staff
And laid way for home and hearth,
Lazy smoke paving the golden light—
Did he have a you, there?

Look at that.
You break your diptych,
You turn into the sun and raise an arm.
There—
The mountains bowing to the meadows
Like a horse to the darkened trough.

Tagus

or The Chariot

Even in the child I knew the man.
He was one of those tyrants of the smash,
With an instinctive calculus for violence.
There are such in every town to the Outer Sea.
They lead packs of other boys to riot and ruin,
Beating dogs in the street and throwing bricks,
Or, if they are noble, devising complex ways
To torture servants or, gods forbid, their tutors.

Such a person dares everything; there is no limit,
And for many other boys this is what nectar
Is to the working bee—a siren pull in the soul
That will drag them across the city, across countries
And into the most horrific broils we can invent,
All for vicinity to this hair-raising He.

Plainly it is a kind of love. What would they not do,
These men and the boys within them, for Alexander?
Nothing, except dishonour themselves in his eyes,
Far better to die (as so many do) and impress him.

The most useful thing I ever taught him was to look
His men in the eyes, and tend them after the battle.
For the harvest was his, not his enemies'. He was Death's
richest fee-farmer and he must pay a rent in tears.

So I imagine him (if he listens to his old master):
He dismounts his horse and stoops to the lowliest soldier
Dying on the field, blanching as the blood leaves him.
Alexander with his gold hair and rough Thracian features
Gifts the man a kiss, a killing one, that makes the soldier
Feel he is in the afterlife already, and so sends him there.

I hope he does this with the reverence it deserves,
That he does not laugh afterwards with Hephaestion
Or his lesser fellows, about the skew of the man's limbs
Or the smell of his insides, or some other ignoble thing.
But I would not put it past him.

An old problem
or The Lovers

To them maybe it was perfect.

They certainly had a conspicuous way
Of ignoring everything else, no other friends,
No after-school anything: just imparadised in each other.

For some there was a slow siren of alarm.
But they were so young it didn't occur to me to think.
I guess I fell for their innocence.

I was still a child myself. I believed in things so easily.

When she told me, my daughter, when I finally had
That conversation, while I pretended to be ironing,
I felt desolate. Twelve years old!

His parents also felt my guilt was warranted,
And as young mothers are so well-versed in it,
I was ready to play my part. Played it well, for a while.

Now, I am older, and so are the key players.

No disaster struck. I'm not a grandmother yet.
When I ask her about back then, she looks wistful,
One more thing she's too young for.

She says it feels like it happened to someone else.
It was like a wonderful dream, and as she got older,
As she woke up, it came apart

Like a cake into butter and eggs and flour.

Life hack

or The Tower

Apt it would end in a fit of pique.
The world, I mean. With plastic tipped
Into the sky, with us staring at our toes
As dead skin is tickled away by premium fishes,
And with a global shortage of wherewithal.
All the good things are nulled by the end
They led to. I worry about the ground
Under the sea, the upset creatures swimming
Backwards, the birds dropping like bombs,
The drone made by the infinite capsize
We've staged on a still sea. If only
A life was longer, or shorter, or shared,
Or more thoughtful, or more trivial,
Less this way inclined—or perhaps that way.

It's easy to find reasons and be wrong,
But what if we were still druids and
Cared most about erecting rocks in fields,
And lying, one night a year, face up
So snicks of light would fret our bare skins?
What if a family still took turns by candlelight
Watching the sheepfold for roaming wolves,
Or spent weeks preserving fruit to stack
In jars in the cool cellar, laying up against
Poor harvests in the better seasons, learning
Trust in tomorrow through the work of today?
Would it be so bad, to put the winnowing fork
Through our lives and find again
The grains, from out this deadly chaff?

Distaff

or Three of Cups

The janky teeth of their cogs,
Machined for lesser grooves,
Scratched up schools and family units,
Making issues and war wherever

Until fate met them up
To notchless sorority.
Just a weird harmony, knolless,
A smooth Bermuda to be lost into

Each other's company, all day at a time.
Three rooms at uni but two vacant.
The world had to be masticated,
Almost too turned over, events, feelings

On the long wend to a consensus,
Nothing was kibosh, all kosher,
Abby emcee, Ali plaintiff, satanic advocate Sammi
On: parents, feminism, politics, boys, other girls

Two taking a turn on the single bed,
The third the carpet, jacket-blanket and jacket-pillow.
Whispers giving out to sleep at three-ish,
Sleep giving out to another dawn of shared breath.

Flâneur
or The Hanged Man

A coke habit and problems with Papa,
Thirty rings on his trunk already
And a bad case of affectation, he'd
Do a line and say: *Splendid.*

The way she hated it! Multi-hyphenate,
Like, hate-love-pity and some hazy
Fourth, a sort of sepia light
That made his shtick into chutzpah.

Fact was, he was an old-school louche,
A back-along soul who got really lost,
Meaning well, getting into scrapes.
It irritated how much wonder he had left.

He'd go to a movie and say, *It's amazing
What they can do*, like a pensioner. He'd
Come inside her and say, *Thank you so
Much*, and squirming she'd kick him out.

At some point they stopped touching for good.
She realised when she told him there was
Sunscreen on his Adam's apple
But didn't reach for the blob herself.

A hot morning on the Staten Island ferry,
He told her he'd seen his own death.
By shotgun, in a forest. She laughed:
Was the guy Dick Cheney? Ha-ha-hmm.

That wasn't the last time she saw him,
But she wondered if it would be. Had
A bad feeling that turned out wrong.
But she knew the last time was coming,
And soon.

Schnozz

or King of Cups

A great nose, bodying forth!
The beak marks character,
Shouts *give way, fall to,*
Spells powers of discernment
More than olfactory, as if
In that upturned chimney
There lived an antiquarian
Played by Javier Bardem
Intoning sophisticated nothings
With a circuit to your head.

Long bridges or rumpling hills,
Both have the whiff and woof of
Sex; both a mind's eye
Might draw in lolling
Circles of lusty picturing.
In men, they say watch out
Below; in women, they say
Watch out below. Length,
Girth, and Skew: all are terrific.
Let them demand a broomstick
And cauldron steaming.

No, the unerring bridge going
Nowhere finds no custom.
Blow overboard those ho-hum
Buttons and binkies, smudged
On and piffled easily away

By passing atishooes
And, *madre mia*, to have a conk
Pruned back, to rhinoplastise . . .
Add a track to the Decalogue
To bracket those bloody barbers,
For a good nose knows its virtue.

Mater familias
or Six of Swords

Her tone was underlined,
But I didn't want to get into it.
The terrain wasn't conducive.

She was shaking the car keys
As if over a baby. There's an
onomatopoeia for it in Spanish . . .
Tintoneo. She was *tintoneando* the keys.

This was hard to bear for reasons
Inarticulable; I was doing anger and
I was doing anxiety. I imagined
The keys falling into a drain.

I loved my mother. I did.
But I used to love her easier.
Now it was a group project
She kept having the worst ideas for.

If I was the baby, I moonlighted therapist.
I could have her nodding at my insights
And sagacities for an hour, then, Bam—
I'd get: You're too young to understand.

Too young? Mum. You may be too old.
I meanwhile am the perfect age. I'm Goldilocks.

It's a matter of perspective: how to reduce them to one.
Because agreeing to disagree is akin to
Locking door after door in a house
Until you're all standing in the broom cupboard
With nothing to say.

By the way, this was about her not letting me
Borrow her car and then, upon long questioning,
Relenting. By which time I said, Forget it.
And then she insisted, and then there was *tintoneo*.

In the end I 'took the L'
(As my own children say)
And borrowed the car.

Her caller

or Seven of Cups

The flies nagging the windows,
The ants militant at the honey,
The tūī monkeying the flowers.
All were witnesses. All said nothing.

Still, I was never alone.
These cameo creatures were there.
They wore a too studied silence
That said they were watching.

It was a fine day in November.
There was a need for sunnies.
The UV felt at least eight
As I bathed nude on the grass.

The earth was keeping my place
In a Mary Renault book of my mother's.
A honeyed crust had fallen off my plate.
I felt lazy without feeling guilty.

I ignored the sound of a car.
A daisy had my attention. Or was it a dandelion?
I wouldn't notice if either went extinct;
They were just words in my head.

A city girl, the car hadn't registered.
But there, at my mother's, it should've. It did.
She lived nowhere, and now she was dead.
I thought this thought backwards.

Then I shot up, like a garden rake
Stepped on in a *Looney Tunes* episode,
Naked and trying not to be.
The car was a Jeep down the drive.

I stood, like Venus in that shell,
Wobbly with a head-rush,
And watched through the gorse
A man getting out. He looked familiar.

He seemed to walk up very slowly,
As if wanting to withhold
The revelation of his identity.
Or, I thought, to withhold mine.

But I was patient. I believed in the fullness of time.
I heard the flies ping the windows and the crunch,
As I stepped towards the man, of my lost toast.
But otherwise my several witnesses stayed silent.

Salt

or Ten of Cups

There I was, wading into the sea,
Carrying the filament of my sanity
Above the waves like a candle.

Ahead, my father lifted
His new baby onto his shoulders
And grimly scanned the horizon.

Behind, a lifeguard, quiet quitting,
Watched everyone sally out
To meet the riptide.

An ill sprite had the run of me that day.
I sharpened knives against myself.
I dreaded the cold water long
Before I made myself walk into it.

Meanwhile my new half-sister,
In an orbit of unalloyed joy
Clapped her hands together,
And looked at the sun.

Her two bodies
or Two of Swords

Glimpse this revenant,
This lady of the lake, this Lazarus,
This totemic self in transports
Of ecstasy, just to be back, to be here.

She was me. The me that I forgot,
That I said I made my peace with forgetting
But that I begged back in the insomniac hours.

Now she is back, she has lifted the veil
As easily as if it were a choice, has torn
The flaming cloth from our foreheads.

This woman I barely know, walking out
Of the water, of my memories, holding two swords:
Her working arms made of my broken ones.
And with sublime reproach she approaches me.

I am taking back this body, she says,
This body you have occupied like a decadent court,
Like overstaying guests exhausting its supplies,
Tearing its arrases down to bare alcoves,
Leaving its lights long out, its sconces empty.
She says, I am taking this body back,
Get out.

Accident
or Eight of Wands

The King of Canaan is run through
With a tent peg, his spiked mind
Matted with the dust.

What clever machines
Are made of dumb particles.
Their purposes weigh nothing.
Their knowledge weighs nothing.
When gone, who can say they were there?
Who can turn the murder weapon back into a peg?

Scoop the king's brain up, by all means.
Take it to the best doctors.
But changes are terminal
And we must run forward
In our animal dumbness.

Regifted

or The Magician

I was one of those children
That keeps the word *precocious* alive,
Smart but with a maturity disorder.
I was one of those children
That thinks factoids as good as cash
At the bank of adult approval.

Talking to me was like flicking between
C-Span and Nickelodeon.
I was half-fluent in Esperanto,
Having thrown a dart at Encarta
And printed out the result.
I knew the Brest-Litovsk but thought
Orgasm was organism in stutter.
My few friends were sufferers, too,
Or in other ways maladapted
To school rituals like rugby, spreading
Rumours and not putting your hand up.

Then I grew up. Then I was defrocked.
It was 23:59 and then it was 00:00.
I was trained and tired:
For nothing.

Justice

or Five of Swords

A torii with a view of the voice,
The gap in his teeth
Sang bonhomie
When he least meant it to,
Like a corpsing extra
In a Great War documentary.
He was once expatiating
On poverty and its effects
When he loosed an A-sharp.

It helped me sympathise.
I had tired of his rightness,
His sharpened moral presence.
He was like a dog holding an egg in its mouth:
You waited for the crunch.

But then he'd squeak, or whistle,
Or just float up an octave and
You felt you'd won a round off him.
It made one smile internally.
It gave feelings of balance.
You were cheered for
Your next postmortem,
Eager for the next stray note.

On fire
or Eight of Swords

The redwoods had blown
Themselves to pieces
In an afternoon.

Blackened bars now jemmied
Into my mother's perfect front lawn
Like needles from some cosmic acupuncturist,

And ash: Ash you had to keep clapping off
Like a gymnast sizing up the vault.

It was a time of new textures,
Grit in your spit and behind your ears.

The insurance company
Asked for patience between two repeated songs:
'Party in the USA' and 'You're So Vain'.

I pictured my mother, just Before, hose in hand,
Spraying down the house, her phone silencing my calls.

While on speaker, I skimmed the oily top off
A pail of water, made a seat where the lounge
Had been, and watched the sun fall into the earth.

The profile

or Four of Swords

That ledge, its two prominences
In latitudes with his eyes and
His dark brows bisecting, or not
Quite—a 40:60 ratio left and right;
And his nose, a personality nose, leaning;
His jaw a romance novel, a Fabio.

It was this last she fell in love with,
She the artist to whom these considerations
Of form, composition and light belong.
And all three were party to her falling.

She had been smoking alone in the dark
Outside her friend's house, and profiled
In the window of a passing car, its internal light on,
This stranger's face: half warm yellow, half black,
Gliding the country night like a will-o'-the-wisp.
She'd wished she were a camera, or a lockbox,
A device for keeping things safe. The car drove on,
The light was flicked off. And she'd looked
Around, jealous that witness be hers alone.

Funny, now, to think of keeping him hers,
When his face was hanging right this minute
In a gallery ten miles away. Funny because he,
This former stranger, was in fact Tomas,
Was a whole, very real, person, whose mind
She now knew almost as well as her own.

Still, though, she drew him,
As she had done later that very night
After, cold and alone, she'd watched the car turn around,
Headlights sweeping back across the fields, towards her.

Companionate
or Four of Wands

They didn't make love
For a long time.
They were busy.

But they still kissed
Goodnight. They still
Held each other very close.

They thought maybe they should
Be dissatisfied, have a lack,
But they didn't. It's not

That sex had gone out
Of their world or minds, it
Wasn't that a colour ebbed.

The colour green, say,
They still saw it. In the trees,
In the bushes, in others' eyes.

But there was no green between
Them, that season. There were
Others, though, many other colours.

Imagine a full English, the breakfast.
One person will make their forkful
Egg, bacon, toast, mushroom, black

Pudding, all at once.
Another person picks two to go at,
Or three. Another tastes one by one.

What a feast, a rainbow,
Is being with the right person
In one season and the next.

There is time for everything
And times for nothing, because
Time is the love they always make.

Penelope

or Nine of Wands

Being a tragic figure is a snap.
You simply adopt the position:
Take two eyes. Add drops of water.
Better: miss, and let them streak off
To represent joys annulled, &c.

It's not enough to just mope about.
You'll look like a jilted teenager,
A wallflower everyone will want
To close the book on.

Instead:
Put on a rally, a turn for the better.
Reward well-wishers with little smiles
As if you might be lured back to life
With the right anecdotes, the right gifts.

Then, dash their hopes.
Look to the window and stare a long time
At the sea. Count gulls if you need to.
Pretend not to hear your interlocutor.

You see, it is all making and unmaking.
To stick, even stasis has to change.
We would go mad in an endless night,
And in an endless day drown
As sure as in a wine-dark sea.

Carve out
or Queen of Pentacles

She was owed more
Than that moiety.

Who apportions,
The torpid morning
From the woken day?

I get up. I get up, and think:
She was owed more.
More than what little she got.

Skinny morsels,
Where's the feast
Moved to?

Handed out days
From the calendar—
She was owed more.

Where do I send my
Letter of complaint?
My alms? Where, now,
Can I send my share?

Good sons

or Five of Wands

The five brothers:
As babes, a threnody;
As boys, a sounder;
As young men, fleet
On their feet, dressing all
Eyes down with their
Great smack of beauty.

The town felt new again
With their shouts and cheers,
The japes, the winks and hijinks.
One played the lute, another pipes.
One sang tenor, one bass;
All were born dancers.

It was the kind of surfeit
That must have signified,
Must have put right some
Misfortune carried forward
In God's long ledgers.
The pairs of twins first,
Then that crowning fifth.
Did God return on interest?

The envious saw a reckoning,
Foretold disasters. But when they came
They were of the ordinary kind.
A sudden illness for the mother,

Who died with her five sons
Constellated round her bedside
Spelling a happy life and end.
For the father, grief and lameness,
A felling of manly strength.

The brothers held each other
And played sad songs until
The whole town mourned.

But in due time up their natures buoyed.
They took again to brace the winds
And healthful waves. They saw cause
To dance, for there was still goodness to life;
There were still five fingers to a hand.

Baby
or The Star

Lithe leveret!
More arms than two
In your mother's fore
Swaddled naked, in fat
& soft bones, hard gazing
At the swish-swash colours
Forming you for you.

It's a lot.

All's new under the sun
& the sun itself is but a kitten
Held by neck in the teeth
Of a stray starry dam.
I am a kind of monkey
& I'm your daddy,
Hello.

Tabernacle

or Page of Pentacles

The egg seemed to promise a new species
Of creation, sequel to the one we had.
We didn't know then it would be him.

It was the colour of volcanic soil.
We took turns warming it between our thighs
Till it was slippery and hard not to drop.

Held up by only the steadiest hands, the sun
Could almost see into it, to the dark knot there.
The children half-blinded themselves with looking.
The sharpest of them asked: could *it* see out?

The egg took on prayers, wishes, and idle gossip
Like a boat takes on water. It lost its plimsoll lines
To the soil after a very long speech by a visiting witch,
Along with shorter ones by your usual village idiots,
And was never lifted again.

Was it dead? Was it awaiting a season we didn't
Have words for? These questions raged like the Long
Fire they claimed burnt deep inside the earth.
There was no way to really tell. But it kept growing.

The village was swept away and rebuilt, it was raided,
Spread out, then shrunk. Its every part was replaced
Many times over, but it kept its name. Finally it sprouted
Steel towers, housing thousands of thousands.

The egg was now so large only its crown was visible
Above the ground, red and vast as a desert,
And smooth and hard as a pearl.

Yet how small he was when he came out!
In all that vast ooze he was only a point of light.
But he was so, so bright.

Gotterdämmerung
or Four of Cups

In the glacier
Forgotten of the suntime
A flower darkest purple.

In the lake
Bones in the shape of a man
Who famished his care.

In the forest
A dog buried not deep
And her uncoiled yellow rope.

What little gets scraped
In a world of curved edges
And bollards and pinioned fingers
And the flat, flat roam of our eyes.

There may as well be no below
If it refuses to float up
And finally mean something.

Querent (II)

I've misjudged you.
The cards—
They told many stories
And none the one I wrote you.

I thought you
Dry as a sandpit,
Filled with little stones
And, dare I say it: dog shit.

I thought you were a boy
With his hands down his pants.
Proud of himself, of being
So very sure.

My dear, I love to be wrong!
You contain so much. You Orlando,
You are a cat with nine lives
And nine tails, and hearts and hearts.

You are now and you are then.
You dance with the head of a pin,
Clicking your heels like needles
Of the long-lost craft.

Or you can. You might choose to.

Let me see your palm.
Your life-line branches
Like a lover's. See?
It's urgent that you see.

Because you can be so promising, one can,
And have nothing come of it.
It's possible to fail yourself,
Your very nature. It's usual.

People put old souls
To young work, wisdom to
Trivia, drive beauty to secrecy
Every day; I see it happen.

But you, my careful boy—
A career? Money? No, the cards
Were mute, short in coins,
And accidents are a myth.

It's a sign.
There are worldly things
And then there are fabrications,
Like tax, bottled water, flat screens.

I'm not making fun. Read right and
You will kill your mother's voice.
You will make love to your father's
Memory, and be so very happy.

You have this weed growing.
Dig it up, follow its little roots,
See where they end and where they start.
Pull them out.

Because you can be as soft
As the sun was, whisked full of air
At the very, very beginning.
You can live the garden life.

There's no single voice.
No fact is binding.
Watch me roll the dice again.
That four: isn't it also one, three, six?

Acknowledgements

Without the careful attention and enthusiasm of the editors at THWUP, particularly Ashleigh Young, this would be a very different and much more faulty collection. Thank you. Any remaining errors are my own.

I'm grateful to Todd Atticus, for being my first reader and first friend. These poems are the happy product of an annus horribilis, and publishing this volume feels like the beginning of a new stage— another stage—together.

The poem 'The spell' was published in a slightly different form on *badapple*. Thanks to the editors.